Contents

D1463845

Say the sounds

j v w y z ch sh th
ng ai ee igh oa oo ar
or ur ow oi er

Wind in Cornwall

This card is from my sister in Cornwall.

CORNWALL

I went surfing today.

There was a good wind!

See you soon.

Kim xxx

Rain in Spain

Gran and Grandad sent me this card from Spain.

Greetings from Spain

Dear Yasmin,

It has been raining hard all week. What a pain!

Gran and Grandad xxx

It can rain in Spain too!

A storm in Denmark

Mum is on a trip to Denmark.

Denmark

We have had such a storm!

There was thunder and lightning all night long.

xxx

A shower in York

Nan sent me this card from York.

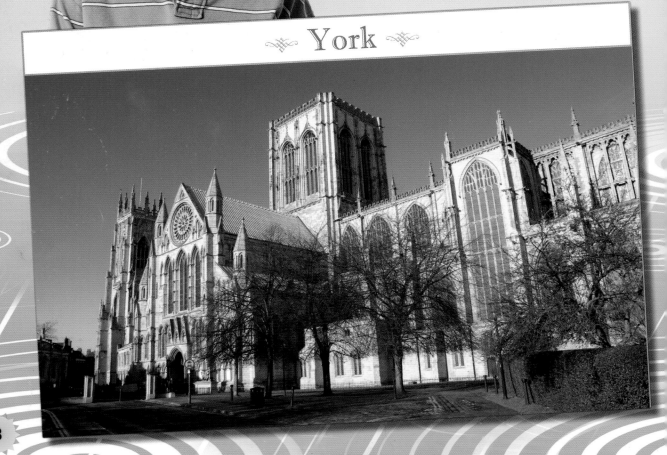

Dear Duncan,

I'm seeing the sights in York.

We just had a shower of rain, and now I am soaking wet!

xxx

A breeze in Scotland

This card is from Mark in Scotland.

Scotland

I went in a boat today.

It was good fun sailing in the breeze!

Mark

Sun in India

My grandad is in India.

It looks very hot!

Greetings from India

Dear Lorna,

It has been boiling hot all week.

Thank goodness for my sun hat!

Grandad xxx

Frost in Finland

This card is from my mum in Finland.

Look at all the snow!

Brrr! It feels like winter today.

There is a hard frost and it is starting to snow.

Mum xxx

Map

Scotland

Finland

Denmark

York

India

Cornwall

Is it hot in India?

Spain